MEETING GOD BIBLE STUDIES

MEETING GOD IN WAITING

Juanita Ryan

*6 studies for individuals
or groups*

IVP

InterVarsity Press
Downers Grove, Illinois

InterVarsity Press
P.O. Box 1400, Downers Grove, IL 60515
World Wide Web: www.ivpress.com
E-mail: mail@ivpress.com

InterVarsity Press® is the book-publishing division of InterVarsity Christian Fellowship/USA®, a student
movement active on campus at hundreds of universities, colleges and schools of nursing in the United States of
America, and a member movement of the International Fellowship of Evangelical Students. For information
about local and regional activities, write Public Relations Dept., InterVarsity Christian Fellowship/USA,
6400 Schroeder Rd., P.O. Box 7895, Madison, WI 53707-7895.

Cover illustration: Roberta Polfus

ISBN 0-8308-2058-2

Printed in the United States of America ♻

15   14   13   12   11   10   9   8   7   6   5   4   3   2   1

10   09   08   07   06   05   04   03   02   01   00   99

Contents

INTRODUCING
Meeting God in Waiting

"How long, Oh God, how long? Will you forget me forever!" This was the cry of the psalmist. It was the cry of many of the prophets. It may also be the cry of your heart at this time in your life. Or it may be that you endured such a time in your past and are left with questions about it. Or you may know someone who is going through such a time.

More than once in our lives we experience waiting through times of uncertainty or times of suffering or times of great need. We are desperate for something to change or for a sign of hope that they will change soon. But nothing happens, nothing changes. If anything, things may get worse. In the midst of such times of waiting it can seem that God is silent. That he has forgotten us. We may be so discouraged that we can't even turn to God for help. Or we may turn to him only to become more frightened and dismayed because our prayers for deliverance go unanswered.

Sometimes our times of waiting are outwardly times of great anticipation. We are planning a wedding. We are expecting a new child in the family. We are preparing for a change of jobs or of location that we very much want to make. But even these times of waiting can be full of anxieties. We may fear that something might go terribly wrong. Or that we are making the wrong decision. Or that we will not be adequate for the task. Or that we will not have the emotional or social skills to weather the adaptation. These fears are often hidden, sometimes even from ourselves. But they can make times of "happy" waiting very difficult. And again we may find inwardly that we are having trouble trusting God to protect and provide for us.

How is it possible to meet God in our times of waiting? How do we meet God when he seems unresponsive to our desperate need? How do we meet God when we find we are having difficulty trusting him with our futures?

The God of the Bible is the God who has promised that he is always with us. Always. Even in our times of waiting. Even when our situation is desperate or our hearts are full of anxiety. Even when we believe he is silent or unresponsive to our need or inattentive to our future. Even when it seems we have lost all faith.

The practice of spiritual disciplines can open the door to transform our times of waiting from times of feeling frightened and even abandoned by God into times of meeting him in new and surprising ways. The disciplines help us focus on God, reflect on our lives, receive support from other believers, quiet our frightened hearts before him, take steps of faith and turn again to God in prayer. The following studies are designed to lead you through a series of spiritual disciplines with the focus on meeting God in times of waiting.

Practicing the Disciplines

Each of the studies focuses on a different spiritual discipline that takes us deeper into the topic.

1. *Scripture study:* we begin with an inductive study that reveals what the Bible has to say about the topic.

2. *Confession:* we look at ourselves in light of Scripture, taking time in the midst of Bible study for silent reflection and repentance.

3. *Community:* we move to interaction with others around a passage or an exercise, asking for guidance and encouragement as we seek God.

4. *Silence:* again we come before Scripture, but this time seeking not to analyze but to hear God's voice and guidance for us.

5. *Obedience:* in light of Scripture's teaching we make commitments to change.

6. *Prayer:* we take time to seek God, weaving prayer through our encounter with Scripture.

These sessions are designed to be completed in 45 minutes to an hour in a group or 30 minutes in personal study. However, feel free to follow the leading of the Holy Spirit and spend as long as is needed on each study.

Every session has several components.

Turning Toward God. Discussion or reflection questions and exercises to draw us into the topic at hand.

Receiving God's Word. A Bible study with application and spiritual exercises.

Now or Later. Ideas that can be used at the end of the study as a time of quiet for a group or individual. Or these ideas can be used between studies in quiet times.

The components of this study can help us meet God with both our minds and hearts. May your times of waiting be transformed into times of hope as God meets you in new ways through these studies.

1

WHEN WAITING IS DIFFICULT

·······································

The Discipline of Scripture Study

We hate to wait. Whether it is being put on hold on the phone or standing in a long line at the store, waiting irritates us.

Sometimes waiting is more than an annoyance. Sometimes waiting is torturous. Waiting for a loved one to come out of surgery. Waiting for the results of a biopsy taken because there is a suspicion of cancer. Waiting for an answer to a prayer we have been praying for months or even years. This kind of waiting is difficult because it is full of fear. We are left in these times with terrible questions about our future. And terrible questions about God.

Scripture gives voice to these times of painful waiting, calling out our anguished fears to God. Wonderfully, Scripture offers us hope and strength for these times of difficult waiting. May this study of Scripture support you in your times of painful and uncertain waiting.

 TURNING TOWARD GOD   *Think of a time when you waited a long time for an answer to prayer. What anxieties did you experience while waiting?

*How did this time of waiting affect your sense of God's presence with you?

The Discipline of Scripture Study
God's Word is one of our greatest resources for knowing him and drawing close to him. What follows is an inductive Bible study that will help you draw out the truths of Scripture for yourself through three types of questions: observation (to gather the facts), interpretation (to discern the meaning) and application (to relate the truths of Scripture to our lives).

 RECEIVING GOD'S WORD   1. Read Psalm 13. How would you title each of the three sections of this psalm (vv. 1-2; vv. 3-4; vv. 5-6)?

2. What do we learn from the first section (vv. 1-2) about how waiting affects the psalmist mentally and emotionally?

3. How does the waiting affect how he experiences God (v. 1)?

4. How does the psalmist's mental, emotional and spiritual experience while waiting compare with your experiences during times of difficult waiting?

5. What does the psalmist ask of God (v. 3)?

6. If God does not answer him, what threats does he face (v. 4)?

7. What does the psalmist commit to doing in the final section of the psalm?

8. What does he reaffirm about God?

9. How might remembering these truths about God help you when waiting is difficult?

10. How can this text be a resource to you in your times of waiting?

11. What would you like to do to find further hope and strength from Scripture in your times of waiting?

Thank God for the resource of his written Word in times of difficulty and especially in times when waiting is difficult.

NOW OR LATER   Using the psalm as a model, journal a prayer. Express to God whatever difficulty you are experiencing. Ask for his help. Reaffirm what you know to be true about who he is, thanking him for the reality of his presence and help in the past, in the future and in the present.

2

WISDOM IN WAITING

·····························

The Discipline of
Confession

One of the ways we might meet God in times of waiting is in using the time to reflect on our values and our choices, and to seek God for wisdom for our lives. Reflecting on Scripture, we compare and contrast God's ways with our ways. We find where we need to acknowledge, through confession, that we have not lived by God's ways. We find areas where we need God to help us.

The verses from Proverbs we will look at are like a conversation of a father to his son, instructing him in wisdom. May you meet God in the wisdom it brings.

 TURNING TOWARD GOD   *If you were to instruct a young man or woman in three or four key points of wisdom for life, what would you focus on?

*Think of a time of waiting in your life. What wisdom did you receive from God during that time?

The Discipline of Confession

God calls us to honesty—honesty with ourselves, with him and with each other. Confession is an opportunity to tell the truth about the ways we have hurt ourselves and others and turned from God's way of love. It is an opportunity to open our hearts and minds for God's Spirit to correct and change us. It is an opportunity to make different, more loving and godly choices each day, one day at a time.

RECEIVING GOD'S WORD 1. Read Proverbs 3:1-12. In these verses a loving dad is sharing basic wisdom for living with his son. What response do you have to the way this father addresses his son?

2. List all of the things the father advises the son to do.

3. What benefits does the father say will come in following this wisdom?

4. Which of the instructions listed are difficult for you to follow?

What makes these particular instructions difficult?

5. In what ways does wisdom sometimes involve waiting?

6. Spend a few minutes contemplating the list. Ask God to remind you of ways you are following these instructions. Write your thoughts about what it seems God is saying to you.

7. Ask God to show you where he would have you change. Write your response to what it seems God is saying to you.

8. Reflect silently. What do you need to confess? Spend some time confessing to God.

9. What change do you want to prayerfully consider making in your life at this time?

10. How might the wisdom in this text help you in times of waiting?

11. In what way do you sense God's presence with you at this time?

Thank God for the forgiveness he offers you.

NOW OR LATER   Focus on one or two of the instructions from this text this week. Each day put it into practice. Make a journal entry at the end of each day about the impact that following this wisdom had on your day.

3

WAITING
WITH SUPPORT
· ·
Practicing the Discipline
of Community

Times of waiting can be very difficult. But waiting with support, rather than waiting alone, can literally make an unbearable situation bearable. One of the ways that God makes his presence known to us in this world is through each other. This can be especially important and powerful in times of difficult waiting. Practicing the discipline of community is like giving ourselves a wonderful gift. As we will see in the following study, it is a gift Paul and Timothy enjoyed in each other.

The Discipline of Community

We were created for relationship with God and with each other. It is in community that we experience love and are given the opportunity to express love. It is in community that we see where our rough edges are and where God is at work in our life. It is in community that we grow into deeper and deeper maturity in Christ. The following exercises and Scripture study are designed to be done with one or two others or in a small group. Ask someone you trust to work through this material with you.

➤ **TURNING TOWARD GOD**   *Imagine yourself waiting for a friend or family member to go through surgery. Picture yourself waiting all alone. What thoughts and feelings come to you as you picture this?

*Now imagine yourself waiting with a supportive friend. What would you want from your friend?

*Picture receiving what you need from your friend as you wait. What thoughts and feelings come to you as you picture this?

*Share your thoughts about these questions with your companion. Take time with your companion to listen to their experiences as well. Explore together the gifts of joy you have received from each other.

RECEIVING GOD'S WORD   1. Read 2 Timothy 1:3-7. This text is the beginning of a personal letter from Paul to Timothy. What words would you use to describe the feelings Paul seems to have for Timothy?

2. What thoughts and feelings do you have in response to the emotional tone of the letter?

3. Paul and Timothy are in a time of waiting to be reunited. What feelings do they each seem to have about their separation?

4. Paul offers Timothy several kinds of support in the letter. First, he tells him very directly how he feels about him (vv. 2-4). How might this have helped Timothy?

5. How might hearing something similar from a friend be of help to you?

6. Paul affirms Timothy's "sincere faith" (v. 5). How might this kind of affirmation be helpful to you?

7. Finally, Paul offers Timothy encouragement. What does he say (vv. 6-7)?

8. What kind of encouragement could you use at this time from a friend?

9. Think of your friendships. How do you offer support to your friends? Think of specific examples of times you have offered or could offer support.

10. How do your friends support you in these ways? Think of specific examples.

11. How might this kind of support from a friend help you to experience God in times of waiting?

12. How has sharing your reflections on this text with a friend or small group enriched your experience of this study?

Pray for each other, thanking God for the gifts of help and support you each receive from the other.

 NOW OR LATER   Write notes to friends during the week, telling them directly how you feel about them and/or offering them words of affirmation and encouragement.

4

WAITING FOR GOD

....

Practicing the Discipline of Silence

In times of silence before God we turn away from the noises in the world around us and from the noises in our heads to hear the voice of the One who loves us without end. As we have seen, times of waiting are often times when it is difficult to experience God's presence, because fears cloud our perceptions. As we release our fears to God and sit quietly before him, our times of waiting can become times of profound experiences of his tender, intimate care for us.

 TURNING TOWARD GOD   *Think of two or three times when you experienced a season of difficult waiting. What sustained your hope during that time?

*What previous experience (if any) have you had with practicing the discipline of silence?

*What hopes and hesitations do you have as you approach this discipline?

The Discipline of Silence

For many of us the disciplines of silence and meditation are the most difficult to pursue. We want to complete a task, read through a book of the Bible or pray through a list of needs. Sometimes, however, God wants us to simply come before him and wait to hear his voice. The Bible study below is best done in quiet, whether you are in a room with others in your small group or alone. Complete all of the questions on your own, then, if you choose, discuss them with a group.

 RECEIVING GOD'S WORD

1. Read Psalm 33:20-22 several times.

> [20]We wait in hope for the LORD;
>   he is our help and our shield.
> [21]In him our hearts rejoice,
>   for we trust in his holy name.
> [22]May your unfailing love rest upon us, O LORD,
>   even as we put our hope in you.

2. Pray for God to guide you in this time.

3. Read the passage again, slowly.

4. What does the psalmist say about waiting and about hope?

5. What does the psalmist say about God?

6. What responses are you experiencing as you let the words of the psalm speak to you?

7. What message does God have for you today?

8. Write a prayer, a poem or a song, or make a collage or drawing which reflects the ways God has met you in your times of waiting.

Allow whatever you have experienced of God in this time to be an ongoing source of hope.

 NOW OR LATER   Spend a few minutes of quiet each morning and each evening this week reflecting on what God showed you of himself as you reflected on Psalm 33.

5

WAITING
FAITHFULLY

·····························

Practicing the Discipline
of Obedience

Sometimes we think of obedience as frenzied activities, as doing much for God. Yet times of waiting are often times when we can do little. For example, waiting to recover from major surgery. Or waiting for a job to open up. Or waiting for God to give us direction about our next stage in life.

It is, ironically, in such times of waiting that we may discover the true meaning of a life of obedience. Because, as it turns out, obedience is not primarily about doing much for God but rather a matter of literally *hanging onto him for dear life*. In John 15 Jesus uses a metaphor to paint a picture of this central truth about obedience. A truth that might help you discover the joy of God's presence in your life in new ways in your times of waiting.

TURNING TOWARD GOD   The central metaphor in the following passage is that of a grapevine and its branches. Allow yourself to picture a thick, strong grapevine with roots deep in rich soil. The vine draws water and nutrients up through its veins to feed its branches so they can thrive. Picture yourself as a branch. Your only way to receive what you need to live and flourish is from the vine. Your one desire, your one work, is to stay attached to the vine so you can drink in its life sustaining nourishment. Now picture the gardener. The gardener loves the vine and its branches and does everything possible to provide the water and nutrients needed to sustain the life of this prized plant. As the gardener feeds the soil, you draw up the nourishment.

What thoughts and feelings do you have in response to this image?

The Discipline of Obedience

Like a good and loving parent, God wants us to stay close by his side so he can guide and teach and care for us. He wants us to walk with him in his way of love so we can know life's deepest joys. This is the call to obedience. As we practice the discipline of obedience and watch God's will unfold in our lives, we will grow in our trust of God's tremendous love for us and our desire to continue this discipline will grow even stronger.

 RECEIVING GOD'S WORD 1. Read John 15:1-12. What does this passage have to say about obedience?

2. What does Jesus say about himself as the vine (vv. 1-8)?

3. What happens when a branch leaves its vine and goes off on its own?

4. What experience have you had of feeling like you were withering spiritually? Describe the situation.

What helped you at that time?

5. What happens when a branch stays close to the vine?

6. What experience have you had of feeling nurtured spiritually? Describe the situation.

7. How might staying closely attached to Jesus and his love help you in times of waiting?

8. What does Jesus say is the relationship between love and obedience (vv. 9-12)?

9. Reflect quietly: What deeper attachment is Jesus inviting you to with himself?

10. What step of further obedience do you want to take in response to the invitation to remain in Jesus' love?

Thank God for his invitation to stay close to Jesus and his love.

NOW OR LATER   Spend some time thinking of other metaphors for staying closely attached to someone who loves you. Choose one of these metaphors and write a poem or prayer or make a drawing or collage using this metaphor to express being closely attached to God.

6

WAITING IN
PRAYER

....

Practicing the Discipline
of Prayer

Prayer is the joining of our hearts and minds and wills to God's. It is certainly petition and confession and thanksgiving. But most fundamentally it is a turning, a coming to God in surrender and trust. When we are faced with difficulties and are waiting for God's help, this surrender and trust can be particularly challenging. It can also be the place where we meet God in new ways.

TURNING TOWARD GOD   Take some time to quiet yourself before God. Reflect on the ways you are able to trust him. Thank him for this trust he has developed in you. Reflect on areas where trust is difficult. Notice the fears that make trust problematic. As you can, name those fears and release them to God, asking him for new gifts of faith and trust. Write about your experience of doing this.

The Discipline of Prayer
Prayer is an opportunity to draw close to God. In prayer we can

express our gratitude, tell him our needs, release our fears and listen for his voice. We may not always feel that we have connected with God, but when we remain faithful to seeking him and listening to him, we will experience the riches of companionship with God.

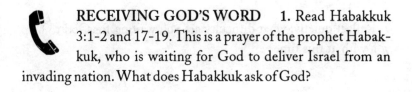 **RECEIVING GOD'S WORD** 1. Read Habakkuk 3:1-2 and 17-19. This is a prayer of the prophet Habakkuk, who is waiting for God to deliver Israel from an invading nation. What does Habakkuk ask of God?

2. What commitment does he make to God (vv. 17-18)?

3. As you look at the list of disasters Habakkuk lists (v. 17), what would be an equivalent list in your life?

4. What would be your natural reaction toward God if this list of disasters happened in your life?

5. In what ways does God help Habakkuk according to verse 19?

6. In your experience what makes it possible to trust God in the face of difficulties?

7. Reflect quietly: what difficulty are you waiting for God to help you with at this time?

8. What do you want to ask of God in this time of waiting?

9. What commitment do you want to make to God?

10. What do you want to remember about who God is?

11. Use your responses to the last four questions to write a prayer.

Ask God to meet you new ways as you wait for him.

 NOW OR LATER   Spend time each day this week repeating the time of prayer in the section "Turning Toward God." Ask God to meet you in new ways each day as you wait for him.

Guidelines for Leaders

My grace is sufficient for you. (2 Corinthians 12:9)

If leading a small group is something new for you, don't worry. These sessions are designed to be led easily. As a matter of fact, the flow of questions in the Bible study portions through the passage from observation to interpretation to application is so natural that you may feel that the studies lead themselves.

You don't need to be an expert on the Bible or a trained teacher to lead a small group discussion. The idea behind these sessions is that the leader guides group members to discover for themselves what the Bible has to say and to listen for God's guidance. This method of learning will allow group members to remember much more of what is said than a lecture would.

This study guide is flexible. You can use it with a variety of groups—student, professional, neighborhood or church groups. Each study takes forty-five to sixty minutes in a group setting.

There are some important facts to know about group dynamics and encouraging discussion. The suggestions listed below should enable you to effectively and enjoyably fulfill your role as leader.

Preparing for the Study

1. Ask God to help you understand and apply the passage in your own life. Unless this happens, you will not be prepared to lead others. Pray too for the various members of the group. Ask God to open your hearts to the message of his Word and motivate you to action.

2. Read the introduction to the entire guide to get an overview of the issues which will be explored.

3. As you begin each study, read and reread the assigned Bible passage to familiarize yourself with it.

4. This study guide is based on the New International Version of the Bible. It will help you and the group if you use this translation as the basis for your study and discussion.

5. Carefully work through each question in the study. Spend time in meditation and reflection as you consider how to respond.

6. Write your thoughts and responses in the space provided in the study guide. This will help you to express your understanding of the passage clearly.

7. It might help to have a Bible dictionary handy. Use it to look up any unfamiliar words, names or places. (For additional help on how to study a passage, see chapter five of *Leading Bible Discussions*, InterVarsity Press.)

8. Consider how you need to apply the Scripture to your life. Remember that the group will follow your lead in responding to the studies. They will not go any deeper than you do.

Leading the Study

1. Begin the study on time. Open with prayer, asking God to help the group to understand and apply the passage.

2. Be sure that everyone in your group has a study guide. There are some questions and activities they will need to work through on their own—either beforehand or during the study session.

3. The flow of each study varies a bit. Many of the studies have time for silent reflection as well as for group discussion. Think through how you will lead the groups through the times of silence, and read through the notes for guidance. It can be very powerful to have times of silence in the midst of a group session. Session four

focuses on silence particularly and calls for an extended time apart. Then you can come together and share your experiences.

4. At the beginning of your first time together, explain that these studies are meant to be discussions, not lectures. Encourage the members of the group to participate. However, do not put pressure on those who may be hesitant to speak during the first few sessions. You may want to suggest the following guidelines to your group.

☐ Stick to the topic being discussed.

☐ Your responses should be based on the verses that are the focus of the discussion and not on outside authorities such as commentaries or speakers.

☐ These studies focus on a particular passage of Scripture. Only rarely should you refer to other portions of the Bible. This allows for everyone to participate on equal ground and for in-depth study.

☐ Anything said in the group is considered confidential and will not be discussed outside the group unless specific permission is given to do so.

☐ Provide time for each person present to talk if he or she feels comfortable doing so.

☐ Listen attentively to each other and learn from one another.

☐ Pray for each other.

5. Have a group member read the introduction at the beginning of the discussion.

6. Every session begins with the "Turning Toward God" section. The questions or activities are meant to be used before the passage is read. These questions introduce the theme of the study and encourage group members to begin to open up. Encourage as many members as possible to participate, and be ready to get the discussion going with your own response.

7. Either prior to or right after "Turning Toward God" you will see a definition of the specific discipline the session focuses on.

Have someone read that explanation.

8. Have one or more group member(s) read aloud the passage to be studied.

9. As you ask the questions under "Receiving God's Word," keep in mind that they are designed to be used just as they are written. You may simply read them aloud. Or you may prefer to express them in your own words.

There may be times when it is appropriate to deviate from the study guide. For example, a question may have already been answered. If so, move on to the next question. Or someone may raise an important question not covered in the guide. Take time to discuss it, but try to keep the group from going off on tangents.

10. Avoid answering your own questions. If necessary, repeat or rephrase them until they are clearly understood. Or point out something you read in the leader's notes to clarify the context or meaning. An eager group quickly becomes passive and silent if they think the leader will do most of the talking.

11. Don't be afraid of silence in response to the discussion questions. People may need time to think about the question before formulating their answers.

12. Don't be content with just one answer. Ask, "What do the rest of you think?" or "anything else?" until several people have given answers to the question.

13. Acknowledge all contributions. Try to be affirming whenever possible. Never reject an answer. If it is clearly off-base, ask, "Which verse led you to that conclusion?" or again, "What do the rest of you think?"

14. Don't expect every answer to be addressed to you, even though this will probably happen at first. As group members become more at ease, they will begin to truly interact with each other. This is one sign of healthy discussion.

15. Don't be afraid of controversy. It can be very stimulating. If you don't resolve an issue completely, don't be frustrated. Move on and keep it in mind for later. A subsequent study may solve the problem.

16. Periodically summarize what the group has said about the passage. This helps to draw together the various ideas mentioned and gives continuity to the study. But don't preach.

17. At the end of the Bible discussion you may want to allow group members a time of quiet to work on an idea under "Now or Later." Then discuss what you experienced. Or you may want to encourage group members to work on these ideas between meetings. Give an opportunity during the session to allow people to talk about what they are learning.

18. Conclude your time together with conversational prayer, adapting the prayer suggestion at the end of the study to your group. Ask for God's help in following through on the commitments you've made.

19. End on time.

Many more suggestions and helps are found in *Small Group Leader's Handbook* and *The Big Book on Small Groups* (both from InterVarsity Press). Reading through one of these books would be worth your time.

Study Notes

Study 1. When Waiting Is Difficult. Psalm 13.

Purpose: To discover how the discipline of Scripture study allows us to meet God in times of waiting.

Question 1. This question gives an overview of the psalm, looking at it as a whole made up of interconnected parts. There are no "right answers" in terms of titling the sections, rather this is an opportunity to read the psalm and to then step back in order to get a general sense about its tone and content.

Question 2. The mental and emotional impact of this time of waiting in the face of great danger is that the psalmist is weary. Mentally he is constantly "wrestling with his thoughts." Emotionally he experiences sorrow every day.

Question 3. Spiritually, this time of waiting is a time of fearing or believing that God has forgotten him. The psalmist feels abandoned by God, forgotten by God, as if he does not matter to God. He must be deeply afraid that God is gone and he will be destroyed by his enemy.

Question 4. Encourage group members to share as freely as they desire about their mental, emotional and spiritual struggles during times of difficult waiting. Realize that everyone's experience will be different. Some people may relate closely to the psalmist's experience. Others may have had times of waiting in the face of a threat or danger and of being comforted by God's presence or by a deep sense of hope. Acknowledge the validity of the range of experiences participants may have had.

Question 5. The psalmist asks God to look at him, to answer him and to "give light to his eyes" so he doesn't die. Because he feels like God has forgotten him or looked away, he asks God to see him, to see his danger, his need, his distress. And because it seems God is not doing anything, he asks God to answer him—to take action on his behalf, to save him from danger. He also asks God to give "light to his eyes," which may be a metaphor for hope, but more likely is a request for direction and help in the face of danger—direction that will allow him to defeat his enemy.

Question 6. The threat the psalmist faces is death. This is not a small threat. And it may be a threat some of the participants have faced themselves or with a loved one in the form of a life threatening illness or some other grave danger.

Question 7. In the final section the psalmist commits to trusting God, to rejoicing in God's help before it comes and to singing to the Lord as he remembers that God has been good to him in the past. This is a huge commitment and not always an easy one to make when there is no immediate sense of God's help or presence. You might want to encourage participants to discuss the struggle involved in making a commitment in this kind of situation.

Question 8. In making the commitment, the psalmist is reaffirming that God's love is unfailing, that God is a God who saves, that God is good—and more specifically that he is good to each of us in response to our very personal needs.

Question 9. Look at each of these truths about God and reflect on them. Imagine the impact each truth would have on their mental, emotional and spiritual well-being in a time of difficult waiting.

Question 10. Encourage participants to allow themselves to be in any one of the phases the psalmist moves through. The passage can be a resource in helping us express our emotional, mental and spiritual distress. It can help us call out to God. It can help us reaffirm our hope in God, reminding us of who he is.

Question 11. Examples would be meditating on this passage from time to time and finding similar texts to meditate on. Or this kind of study can be used to explore a variety of texts from Scripture to see what the Bible says about waiting.

Study 2. Wisdom in Waiting. Proverbs 3:1-12.

Purpose: To practice the discipline of confession, deepening our awareness of God with us in times of waiting.

Question 1. The purpose of this question is to allow participants to be drawn into the text, as if this father were addressing them. The tone seems loving: the father says "my son," and he clearly desires the good benefits of wise living for his son. There is no sense of accusation, disrespect or control, but a clear, loving sharing of wisdom.

Question 2. The purpose of listing all the advice given in these twelve verses is to ferret them out from the text so participants can look at each piece of wisdom and the list as a whole.

Question 3. This is another listing—this time of the benefits of wise living. Again this listing is for the purpose of seeing all that is being said here and of seeing the relationship between wise living and the benefits that can come from these choices.

Question 4. Encourage participants to reflect on the list they made in response to question 2. Encourage honesty. It is difficult for all of us at times to trust the Lord or to remember to not go off on our own steam.

Question 5. Encourage the group to give examples of times when wisdom might mean waiting. Explore with the group how realizing this truth might ease the stress of waiting.

Question 6. Give the group time to do this individual work. Let the group know that you will not ask them to share their response to this reflection with the group, unless they want to. This reflection is important, however, because seeing and acknowledging the work of God in us is vital for our own encouragement.

Questions 7-10. These three questions are very personal and need to be grouped together as an individual exercise in confession. Give participants the time and space needed to do this (probably about twenty minutes). When the group comes back together, it may be a powerful experience to read out loud 1 John 1:9 and to lead the group in a simple prayer of thanksgiving for God's love and forgiveness. Then you can reflect together on your experience of confession.

Question 11. This text is about seeking God for direction. This is crucial wisdom for our times of waiting. Discuss personal ways this might help in times of waiting.

Study 3. Waiting with Support. 2 Timothy 1:3-7.
Purpose: To experience God-with-us in times of waiting, through the support of community.

Turning Toward God. If you are leading a small group, ask group members to complete this portion with a friend prior to small group, and then reflect on what you have learned together at the beginning of your meeting. Or give a time of quiet to complete the first three questions, and then pair off and take ten minutes to complete the questions together.

Background. Paul and Timothy were quite close as friends and coworkers. Paul had left Timothy in Ephesus to provide leadership in Paul's absence. In his first letter to Timothy, Paul says he expects to see Timothy soon. But by the time this second letter was written, Paul is in prison in Rome. So Timothy needs encouragement for many reasons. He is certainly concerned for Paul and misses Paul a great deal. He is fairly young to be in a leadership position. He must have been counting on Paul's return for personal support and for support in the challenges of leadership. (*International Standard Bible Encyclopedia*, [Grand Rapids, Mich.: Eerdmans, 1988].

Question 1. This question helps us enter into the experience of this letter from Paul to Timothy, as if it is a letter we have received from a friend. The emotional tone of the letter is loving, tender, intimate, grateful, direct.

Question 2. Group members may have a variety of responses to this emotional intimacy. Give individuals the freedom to share whatever their response might be—whether it is surprise or discomfort or distrust or being deeply moved.

Question 3. Paul's response to their separation includes gratitude for Timothy, constantly thinking about him, praying for him and longing to see him. Timothy's response to the separation was that of tears.

Question 4. Encourage participants to reflect on how these direct expressions of intimate love from Paul to Timothy might have helped Timothy in this time of grieving over their separation and of waiting to be together again.

Questions 8-12. The purpose of these questions is to allow participants to reflect on the friendships in their lives and to explore how they might give and receive the kind of loving support Paul offered Timothy in this letter. We give and receive support through affirmation and direct statements about the value of a person as an individual and as a friend.

Study 4. Waiting for God. Psalm 33:20-22.
Purpose: To discover through the discipline of silence the possibility of knowing God's presence in times of waiting.
General Note. If you are leading a group, consider meeting in a setting that will allow you to separate for quiet reflection—for example, at a church or in a quiet park. Open with prayer and

perhaps some worshipful singing. Then allow forty-five minutes to an hour to work through the material in "Turning Toward God" and "Receiving from God." Encourage people to find a place of privacy and take time to write in their responses to the questions. Then simply sit in silence, listening to and reflecting on God. If the group chooses to stay together for some of their experience in silence, allow time to do so. Then come together to talk about what you experienced and how God spoke through the passage.

Background. Psalm 33 is a call to God's people to praise him for who he is—our loving, powerful Creator and Lord. It is also a call to acknowledge our dependence on God. Verses 20 to 22 are the people's response to this call.

Study 5. Waiting Faithfully. John 15:1-12.

Purpose: To discover God in new ways during times of waiting, through the discipline of obedience.

Question 1. This question looks at the text from a broad perspective before looking more closely at the specifics. The heart of this text is that God's call to obedience is a call to "remain in God's love." To obey God is to love. To love is to obey God. This always means "hanging onto Jesus for dear life," staying deeply attached to him and to his love for us and all others.

Question 2. Jesus tells us he is the true vine. He says he wants us to stay close to him. He says we are to remain in him and that he will remain in us.

Question 3. Jesus paints a clear picture of our true dependence on him. We cannot live without him. We cannot bear the fruit of love without him. We literally wither and die without him.

Question 4. Encourage the group to share experiences they have had trying to live a spiritual life on their own without an acknowledged, active dependence on Christ.

Question 5. When we stay close to the Vine, we bear the fruit of love, we know ourselves to be deeply loved, we are "trimmed clean" by the Father, and we come to know joy.

Question 7. Times of waiting can be times of gaining new perspective. As suggested in the brief introduction to this study, times of waiting may be times when we learn a whole new meaning of the word *obey*. In times of waiting our obedience may be that of seeking God more deeply, more urgently. It may be that of knowing ourselves to be deeply, powerfully held by his love. It may be that of turning to him over and over again every day. Obeying God may be a matter of holding on to him for dear life and in this way learning an entirely new way of life in our season of waiting.

Questions 9-10. Spend five or ten minutes in silence, reflecting on these questions. Then allow time for any to share whatever they may want from this time. Pray for each other.

Study 6. Waiting in Prayer. Habakkuk 3:1-2, 17-19.
Purpose: To experience the resource of prayer in our times of waiting.

Question 1. He is asking God for miraculous, awesome deeds to be done on behalf of his people. They are in need of help and deliverance. Habakkuk knows what God has done for Israel in the past, and he is asking for God to act with power again.

Question 2. Habakkuk makes the commitment that no matter what, no matter how difficult things become, he will trust God and find joy in God, remembering that God is Savior.

Question 3. Encourage people to make a personal, modernized version of this list. Have the group share their paraphrase of verse 17 with each other.

Question 4. Most of us would experience a variety of reactions to God if a series of disasters happened in our lives. We would probably feel discouraged about life and our relationship with God. We might be afraid we had been forgotten or abandoned by God. We might be afraid we were being punished by God. We might react in anger at God.

Question 6. Trusting God in the face of life's difficulties does not come easily or naturally. But there are things that can help. Being understanding and compassionate with ourselves for our struggles and difficulties with trusting can be helpful. Identifying our fears and reactions in relation to God, and talking to God about our feelings can be helpful. The support of other believers who are compassionate with our pain may help. Remembering what we know to be true of God can help. Asking God to show himself in the midst of the difficulty can also be helpful.

Questions 7-10. Give five or ten minutes for each person to reflect on these questions personally. Then you may want to discuss these questions or you may want to simply move on to question 11.

Question 11. If you are leading a group, give people time to write their prayers, and then allow each person to pray aloud.